HOW TO OVERCOME LONELINESS

Hope for the heart

Sydney Dikwi

KINGDOM BOOKS
Your kingdom come, your will be done

Copyright © Sydney Dikwi, 2015

Published by Kingdom Books, an imprint of *CreativeJuicesBooks*, *Singapore (www.creativejuicesbooks.com)*

All rights reserved. No part of this book may be reproduced, stored in a retrieval system, or transmitted in any form or by any means — electronic, mechanical, digital, photocopy, recording, or any other — except for brief quotations in printed reviews, without prior permission in writing from the publisher.

All Scripture quotations, unless otherwise indicated, are taken from the *Holy Bible: New International Version* ®. Copyright © 1973, 1978, 1984 International Bible Society. Used by permission of Zondervan Bible Publishers. All rights reserved.

Scripture quotations marked *AMP* are taken from the *Amplified® Bible*, copyright © 1954, 1958, 1962, 1964, 1965, 1987 by The Lockman Foundation. Used by permission.

Scripture quotations marked *NKJV* are taken from the *New King James Version®*. Copyright © 1982 by Thomas Nelson. Used by permission. All rights reserved.

Scripture quotations marked *NLT* are taken from the *Holy Bible, New Living Translation*, copyright © 1996, 2004, 2007 by Tyndale House Foundation. Used by permission of Tyndale House Publishers, Inc., Carol Stream, Illinois 60188. All rights reserved.

Scripture quotations marked *ASV* are taken from the *Holy Bible: American Standard Version*.

Scripture quotations marked *KJV* are taken from the *Holy Bible: King James Version*.

National Library Board, Singapore Cataloguing-in-Publication Data

Name: Dikwi, Sydney, author.
Title: How to overcome loneliness: hope for the heart/Sydney Dikwi
Other titles: Hope for the heart
Description: Singapore: Kingdom Books, [2015]
Identifiers: OCN 925687629 | ISBN 978-981-09-7314-8 (paperback)
Subjects: LCSH: Loneliness--Religious aspects-- Christianity. | Christian life.
Classification: LCC BV4911 | DDC 248.86--dc23

Cover design by Karin Skold

Contents

Preface v

1. Understanding Loneliness 1
2. Types of Loneliness 10
3. Loneliness Is Different from Depression 17
4. Common Feelings of Loneliness 29
5. Causes of Loneliness 40
6. Loneliness Is Different from Solitude 49
7. You Are Not Alone 57
8. How to Overcome Loneliness 68

Prayer to Jesus 99

This book is dedicated to the author of *A Call to Alignment*, Apostle Kuda Mupfeka Snr, of Centre of Hope Ministries (South Africa), who helped me to release and fulfill my calling in ministry. Thanks for being a great father who helped to instill Christian principles in my life. Thanks for not giving up on me and for being a shepherd, tutor, coach, teacher and counselor to me.

PREFACE

Loneliness is an emotional dysfunction suffered by many today. The goal of writing this book is to help readers receive healing from God for their loneliness. This is achieved through the Holy Spirit removing the sting of loneliness from their hearts.

This book enables you to see life in a different way, and gets you ready to move on to new beginnings, new friends and new relationships. It is a great tool that can be used to bring hope to the hopeless. Through simple, yet insightful writing, it points everyone to the ultimate solution for loneliness—intimacy with God and a personal relationship with Jesus Christ.

Pastor Sydney Dikwi

Chapter 1

Understanding Loneliness

"I lie awake; I have become like a bird alone on a roof."

Psalm 102:7

No one likes to feel alone. Deep down inside, all of us desire to be loved and to be with other people. One of the earliest comments God made after He created man was that "It is not good for the man to be alone." (*Genesis 2:18*) The Old Testament Hebrew word translated here as "alone" has negative connotations: it means to be "apart, barred (from others), only, or by oneself".

Loneliness refers to the emotional state of feeling rejected and desolate. It is often accompanied by a sense of hopelessness.

Many times we feel all alone even when we are around other people. Satan often uses these negative emotions to make us feel as if even God has distanced Himself from us. We can identify with the Psalmist David when he cried out:

> My God, my God, why have you forsaken me? Why are you so far from saving me, so far from the words of my groaning?
>
> *Psalm 22:1*

It is natural to feel deep loneliness when you are experiencing a traumatic loss or change in your life. But if you indulge in self-pity and become angry at God, blaming Him for your circumstances, you will start to feel separated from Him and will fail to receive His loving comfort. Instead, you need to seek God even more earnestly at such times, calling out to Him as the Psalmist David did.

This was David's cry to God:

> Turn to me and be gracious to me, for I am lonely and afflicted.
> *Psalm 25:16*

God's Word has much to say about loneliness. If you are feeling lonely today, consider taking a prescription from the Word of God:

> For everything that was written in the past was written to teach us, so that through endurance and the encouragement of the Scriptures we might have hope.
> *Romans 15:4*

God has said that He will never leave us nor forsake us (*Hebrews 13:5*). Even though you walk through the valley of the shadow of death, you shall fear no evil, for God will be with you; His rod and His staff will comfort you (*Psalm 23:4*).

The Lord is close to the brokenhearted and saves those who are crushed in spirit (*Psalm 34:18*). He heals the brokenhearted and binds up their wounds (*Psalm 147:3*).

The Bible is God's instruction manual for life. It provides the answers we need to go through life and gives us comfort, peace and hope for a brighter tomorrow. God inspired it to be profitable and beneficial for us.

> All Scripture is inspired by God and is useful to teach us what is true and to make us realize what is wrong in our lives. It corrects us when we are wrong and teaches us to do what is right.
>
> *2 Timothy 3:16*

Symptoms of Loneliness

Here are some symptoms of loneliness:

- You feel disconnected from people and not accepted or appreciated by them;

- You would rather sit in a corner alone than talk to someone, call a friend, or socialize with others;

- You feel that you are unworthy of other people's love and attention;

- You often blame others for your unfavorable circumstances;

- You avoid communicating with other people in order to avoid conflict—even when that means also avoiding relationships with them;

- You continue to argue in your head or silently to yourself for hours or days, even after the actual argument with the other person is over;

- You have a negative attitude towards life;

- You constantly suffer from lack of energy (you find it hard to get up in the morning as you always feel too tired).

Only God Can Satisfy Us

Being human, we all want to feel loved; and, when we do not feel loved, we often make unwise decisions in our desperate hunt for love. Yet, if we look to God for that love, we will always find it and we will always know we are not alone.

> I have set the Lord always before me. Because he is at my right hand, I will not be shaken.
>
> *Psalm 16:8*

Are you a single person trying to find someone to marry because you are lonely? That is a recipe for disaster. A husband or wife is not a solution to loneliness. If it were, then millions of married people would be happy in their marriages today. But instead many are sinking deeper and deeper into loneliness while in their married state, which they had assumed to be the answer to their loneliness.

Never marry someone in order to ease your pain; rather, address the cause of your loneliness first before you think of accepting someone into your life. It is possible to marry and still feel lonely and empty inside. That void inside you can only be filled by two people cooperating together: God and you alone. If you are lonely, Jesus Himself has given you an invitation you should not refuse.

This is what He says:

"If anyone hears my voice and opens the door, I will come in and eat with him, and he with me."

Revelation 3:20

You can be surrounded by people all the time and still feel lonely, but the Bible says we are never truly alone if we believe in God. He is always there for us, no matter what happens. He stands by our side, even when we cannot feel Him.

When you pass through the waters, I will be with you; and when you pass through the rivers, they will not sweep over you.

When you walk through the fire, you will not be burned; the flames will not set you ablaze.

Isaiah 43:2

Healing for Loneliness

My purpose in writing this book is not to help you forget your loneliness—which may have been caused by a hurtful or traumatic experience—but rather to help you receive healing for it; this is where the Holy Spirit will have to remove the sting that caused the loneliness in the first place. This will enable you to look back upon the healed wound and see it in a different light, because it has been healed and you are no longer lonely but ready to move on and make new friends.

> For God alone my soul waits in silence; from Him comes my salvation.
>
> *Psalm 62:1-2 (AMP)*

Your soul should wait only upon God in times of loneliness and silently submit to Him; for your hope for healing is from Him. If you make God your Rock and your Salvation, surely you shall not be moved (*Psalm 62:5*). If you wait for a human being to fill the void in your heart, you will be disappointed.

Chapter 2

Types of Loneliness

There are various prescriptions to deal with different kinds of loneliness. Make sure you know your problem before you try to fix it.

Interpersonal Loneliness

This type of loneliness occurs when someone who was close to you is separated from you. It is closely associated with grief; you are lonely because of the void left by this person.

The loneliness you feel after the death of a loved one is unlike any other type of loneliness. It is not just *social loneliness,* where you are stuck in your room without friends but you know you can leave your room to go and be with them. It is not *existential or cultural loneliness*, where you do not have the ability to reach out to touch people, but at least you know that they are there.

When a loved one dies, your relationship with that person can never be restored. Death has produced an empty hole in your life and no one can fill that hole except the one who is gone.

Others may become your friends, but they are not the same as the one who is gone. You may marry again, but you will never have the same relationship with the second spouse as you did with the first.

Since death is inevitable and final, you must move on and fill the void in your heart; no one can do it for you. The solution to this type of loneliness is to form new and meaningful relationships.

Social Loneliness

We usually experience social loneliness when we are cut off from our family or a community that we feel is necessary or important to our well-being or survival.

In our loneliness, we can become more vulnerable to temptations that cause us to sin. Loneliness itself is not sin, but when you give in to it and pay it unnecessary attention, you are giving the devil a foothold (*Ephesians 4:27*).

Sometimes the people closest to us can abandon us and leave us lonely. This is not easy for our hearts. But even if your father and mother abandon you, the Lord will hold you close (*Psalm 27:10*). God is a friend who sticks closer than a brother (*Proverbs 18:24*).

God recognized Adam's need for contact with another human being, a need God had built into him. More than just a fellow inhabitant of Eden, Eve would be the object of Adam's love and would love him in return. She would share the wonders of creation as well as the responsibilities of stewardship with him.

Today, however, it is the norm for us to leave family and friends behind as we pursue our educational and vocational goals. First we leave for college, where we usually build new friendships. But those do not last either; when our studies end, we move on again.

Each time we move, we travel alone, leaving old relationships behind. We need to reach out and build new relationships at every juncture. But most times we are more focused on our educational or career goals than we are on our personal relationships, so the task of making friends always ends up at the bottom of the to-do list. And nothing at the bottom of the to-do list ever gets done.

Many of us have no close friends, we are unmarried, and we live lives that feel empty and bleak. *Community* and *family* have become foreign words. We place a low value on *community* because we do not really understand what community is all about anymore.

We are lonely because we have put our careers ahead of our relationships. We can solve this loneliness by realizing the important of relationships and finding ways to reconnect with our families and communities. They are important to us because strong relationships with our family and community members will give us self-worth.

Culture Shock

You experience this type of loneliness when people in a new setting reject you or you find yourself unable to relate with them. Everything seems different and you just can't get comfortable in this new setting. There are people around you, but you are unable to form core relationships with them.

> My friends and companions avoid me because of my wounds; my neighbors stay far away.
>
> *Psalm 38:11*

God designed human beings with a natural need to be loved. As children, we learned to give and receive affection, and we were taught skills that would help us find acceptance in society. Through our relationships with our families, friends, co-workers and others, we form our sense of uniqueness and find our place in life. It is when that need for affection and fellowship goes unfulfilled that we become restless, unhappy and lonely. This type of loneliness is related to *cosmic loneliness* and the solution is similar.

Cosmic Loneliness

Cosmic loneliness sets in when we begin to doubt our self-worth and feel that we do not measure up or cannot achieve complete intimacy or relationship with others. The problem is solved when we see ourselves as accepted by God and we know that we are special to Him.

Psychological Loneliness

This happens when past traumas have hurt us and, afraid of getting hurt again, we separate ourselves from God and from people, or we reject their friendship. We "attach wounds" to our psyche, and these "wounds" will not let us form new relationships. To break free from this type of loneliness, we need to be healed and reconnected with God and people.

Chapter 3

Loneliness Is Different from Depression

Loneliness is not the same as depression. Lonely people feel sorry for themselves; they are sad and miserable. Depressed people have given up and just do not care about anything; they do not even care that they are alone. Lonely people shed a tear; depressed people are beyond tears, they have deeper hurts that are beyond the help of tears.

Lonely people can be helped because potentially they want a better life; they want a core relationship with someone. Depressed people have given up; they want to be alone because nothing matters anymore, and many just sleep all day.

Loneliness is self-rejection, whereas depression is a clinical condition that can be alleviated with medication. Depression is a mental illness characterized by low spirits, weariness, insomnia or hypersomnia, and a lack of interest in any activity. Someone who is depressed might not necessarily feel lonely. Moreover, even people with many friends and loved ones can become depressed too.

Depression can cause a person to withdraw from family and friends. People who suffer from depression no longer desire to be around those they had once been close to, and they also lose interest in activities they had previously enjoyed. Depression is caused by both genetic and environmental factors.

Feeling lonely is different from feeling depressed. Though we cannot conclude that one causes the other, we can say that loneliness and depression are interrelated.

Depressed people often have great difficulty expressing any kind of anger. Instead of becoming angry with the person who has provoked them, their anger is turned inwards against some part of themselves. They do not kick the physical object; instead, they kick themselves. Their anger smolders beneath the surface and usually finds an indirect avenue for expression.

They make everything their own fault; no matter what happens, they always blame themselves. Accepting (as opposed to denying) the fact that one is depressed is a huge first step to resolving the problem.

Symptoms of Depression

- You feel sad and lonely;

- You feel irritable for no good reason;

- You feel tired and drained of energy all the time;

- You suffer from low self-esteem;

- You feel excessively self-critical and worthless;

- You feel disinterested in everything and everyone;

- You find it difficult to concentrate on anything (for example, your work);

- You feel inexplicably weary or find yourself inexplicably weeping for no good reason;

- You undergo changes in your eating patterns: for example, eating too much or losing your appetite;

- You have lost weight in an unhealthy way;

- You experience changes in your sleep patterns: for example, wanting to sleep much or not at all, or not sleeping due to insomnia;

- You complain about vague physical ailments like headaches, backaches or any unexplained number of aches and pains;

- You feel empty, hollow, lifeless and dead;

- You communicate less with others than before;

- You exhibit withdrawn behavior;

- You experience a nervous breakdown;

- You display exaggerated excitement (you try very hard to appear happy).

If these symptoms apply to you, you might be suffering from depression. You need to seek medical treatment and counselling to help you deal with it.

Lonely? You Are Not Alone!

Loneliness is universal. Loneliness is real and it hurts. There is no cure for it, but there is help to deal with it. We can suffer from loneliness in various ways:

- Yearning to see, hear and touch those no longer with us;

- Feeling the loss of attachment and needing to feel that deep connection once again with the beloved;

- Feeling defenseless and unable to manage life's challenges without the beloved;

- Feeling isolated and afraid of forming new bonds, believing that attachments lead to pain;

- Fearing to be alone, yet feeling the need to avoid others.

Loneliness is nothing new. Great men of God, and even Jesus Himself, have all experienced loneliness. The Bible tells us that the Prophet Elijah fled from Queen Jezebel upon hearing that she had vowed to put him to death (because he had defied her orders and continued to worship the true God). Elijah fled into the wilderness and cried out to God that he was all alone, the only one left worshiping Him. He even wanted to end his life.

> But he himself went a day's journey into the wilderness, and came and sat down under a broom tree. And he prayed that he might die, and said, "It is enough! Now, LORD, take my life, for I *am* no better than my fathers!"
>
> *1 Kings 19:4 (NKJV)*

He cried out, "I alone am left; and they seek to take my life." (*1 Kings 19:10, NKJV*) God, however, made it plain to Elijah that he was not alone. He reassured the prophet:

> "Yet I have reserved seven thousand in Israel, all whose knees have not bowed to Baal, and every mouth that has not kissed him."
>
> *1 Kings 19: 18 (NKJV)*

David—giant-slayer, king and psalmist—also experienced profound moments of loneliness: when he was on the run, hunted by King Saul and later in his life by his own son. Many of the Psalms that he wrote expressed his deep loneliness as he cried out to God, pleading for mercy, comfort and help when he felt abandoned and alone.

Jesus, too, has suffered from loneliness. When He was being persecuted, beaten and nailed to the cross, it was the most painful time of His earthly life. He felt that God had abandoned him. And His most faithful followers, too, abandoned him in His hour of need. The people who followed and loved Him before he was crucified were no longer there for him. Jesus knows exactly what it feels like to be alone, and so He knows exactly what you are going through when you feel lonely.

Therefore, since we have a great high priest who has gone through the heavens, Jesus the Son of God, let us hold firmly to the faith we profess.

For we do not have a high priest who is unable to sympathize with our weaknesses, but we have one who has been tempted in every way, just as we are —yet was without sin.

Let us then approach the throne of grace with confidence, so that we may receive mercy and find grace to help us in our time of need.

Hebrews 4:14-16

Jesus experienced loneliness, not just because He felt that His Father had forsaken him when He was on the cross, but also because His disciples forsook Him in His greatest hour of need. Jesus has felt every human emotion, and He knows what it is like to be lonely. Talk to Him about how you feel. For God created us and all of our emotions, so He surely understands us.

> For thou didst form my inward parts: Thou didst cover me in my mother's womb.
>
> I will give thanks unto thee; for I am fearfully and wonderfully made: Wonderful are thy works; and that my soul knoweth right well.
>
> My frame was not hidden from thee, when I was made in secret, and curiously wrought in the lowest parts of the earth.
>
> Thine eyes did see mine unformed substance; and in thy book they were all written, even the days that were ordained for me, when as yet there was none of them.
>
> How precious also are thy thoughts unto me, O God! How great is the sum of them!
>
> *Psalm 139: 13-17 (ASV)*

Loneliness Is Different from Depression

Many people suffer from loneliness in our society—and that includes many Christians, both single and married. Some are lonely because they have lost their spouses through death. Others who still have their spouses with them are left alone when the other partner works extra-long hours or travels frequently to distant places.

Young people often suffer from loneliness when they cannot make or keep friends. Children also feel lonely when they do not receive enough affection from their parents. People with disabilities suffer loneliness, too, because they are unable to get out into society.

Christian singles are lonely, mainly because they envy the world going out two by two, and they feel left out of the game. Most of the time, their loneliness is triggered by the media or the wrong conceptions they have of marriage.

Marriage is God's solution for sexual immorality, and not a painkiller for loneliness or an easy way out for the lonely.

This is what the Apostle Paul has to say to singles; marriage fulfills sexual needs but it is not necessarily the cure-all for loneliness:

> Now to the unmarried and the widows I say: it is good for them to stay unmarried, as I am. But if they cannot control themselves, they should marry, for it is better to marry than to burn with passion.
>
> *1 Corinthians 7:8-9*

Chapter 4

Common Feelings of Loneliness

Loneliness can result in a sick feeling of being left out of the crowd or being unwanted. Some people might feel lonely from time to time, but for others it is a daily way of life. Those who suffer from constant loneliness often feel cut off from other people and might totally lack meaningful contact with anyone at all.

Lonely people have an intense longing to be needed and wanted by someone else. Many of them wear the effects of their loneliness on their faces, which often show a sad countenance or dejected look:

> A happy heart makes the face cheerful, but heartache crushes the spirit.
>
> *Proverbs 15:13*

> A cheerful heart is good medicine, but a crushed spirit dries up the bones.
>
> *Proverbs 17:22*

In the final stages of loneliness, sufferers tend to withdraw from others. In the advanced stages, some try to escape from their loneliness through alcohol, drugs, sex or other forms of entertainment.

Loneliness can afflict anyone from time to time. On many occasions, great men of the Bible have spoken of being alone and feeling the pain of loneliness.

The Pain of Loneliness

Loneliness is painful. It is an aching pain that includes sorrow, sadness, depression, brokenness, hurt, and feeling torn out. Loneliness can lock you in a prison of pain so intense that you are unable to relate to anyone else. At times, you do not know what is worse: physical pain that pulsates through your body or the emotional pain from broken relationships. No matter what the cause, pain binds you to the problem of loneliness so that there is no relief.

> Even in laughter the heart may ache, and joy may end in grief.
> *Proverbs 14:13*

Feeling Lost and Lonely

Lonely people often feel lost, confused, and lacking a sense of direction. They describe their experience of being lost as "darkness; night; blindness; cluelessness; lack of meaning in life". Even the heroes of the Bible have talked about this experience of darkness in their times of loneliness:

> You have put me in the lowest pit, in the darkest depths.
> *Psalm 88:6*

> He has blocked my way so I cannot pass; he has shrouded my paths in darkness.
> *Job 19:8*

You have taken my companions and loved ones from me; the darkness is my closest friend.

Psalm 88:18

Feeling Empty

Lonely people often feel empty inside; there is an aching void in their hearts. Often, they have this emptiness in them because they have lost a loved one. This could have happened, for example, when they broke up with someone special to them. They might still be feeling intense pain as they long to be close to this person; or they might feel cold and empty of all emotion after losing the loved one.

A Persistent Feeling

Loneliness can persist. You can be afflicted with loneliness for a long time and not be able to find a remedy. Such persistent feelings of loneliness can drive sufferers to despair, as they feel overwhelmed and about to break apart at any time. It is like blowing a balloon past its normal capacity, to the point where it is about to burst.

> And now my life ebbs away; days of suffering grip me.
>
> *Job 30:16*

> The churning inside me never stops; days of suffering confront me.
> I go about blackened, but not by the sun; I stand up in the assembly and cry for help. I have become a brother of jackals, a companion of owls...
>
> *Job 30:27-29*

Feeling Imprisoned

Some individuals have no control over their loneliness and feel imprisoned by it. This type of loneliness has its roots in childhood experiences, rejection or abandonment, where the object of love is gone. Sometimes this leads to anger, which opens the door for a spirit of fear and resentment to enter the person. This is why many people imprisoned by their loneliness also harbor a lot of bitterness.

> Set me free from my prison, that I may praise your name.
>
> *Psalm 142:7*

Desiring Death

Loneliness can drive people to desire death. In Chapter 3, we saw how Elijah had prayed to God to end his life because he thought he was all alone, the only one left of God's prophets (*1 Kings 19: 4, 10*). In his loneliest, darkest moments, Job desired death too:

> So that I prefer strangling and death, rather than this body of mine.
>
> *Job 7:15*

In extreme cases, loneliness can even drive people to commit suicide.

And when Ahithophel saw that his counsel was not followed, he saddled his ass, and arose, and gat him home, unto his city, and set his house in order, and hanged himself; and he died…

2 Samuel 17:23 (ASV)

And it came to pass, when Zimri saw that the city was taken, that he went into the castle of the king's house, and burnt the king's house over him with fire, and died.

1 Kings 16:18 (ASV)

There is no doubt that suicide is a terrible tragedy. For a Christian, it is an even greater tragedy because it is a waste of a life that God had intended to use in a glorious way. God is the author of life; thus, the giving and taking of life ought to remain in His hands. Suicide is not the way out of your problems; rather, you should look to Jesus Christ as the answer.

> For this purpose the Son of God was manifested, that he might destroy the works of the devil.
>
> *I John 3:8 (KJV)*

> Thanks be to God, who gives us the victory through our Lord Jesus Christ.
>
> *1 Corinthians 15:57 (NKJV)*

To feel alone and unloved hurts terribly, but loneliness does not have to be a dead end street for you. God understands your feelings, for He Himself has suffered the same loneliness through His Son Jesus Christ.

> And about the ninth hour Jesus cried out with a loud voice, saying, "Eli, Eli, lama sabachthani?" that is, "My God, My God, why have You forsaken Me?"
>
> *Matthew 27:46 (NKJV)*

For we do not have a high priest who is unable to sympathize with our weaknesses, but we have one who has been tempted in every way, just as we are—yet was without sin.

Hebrews 4:15

Life is full of times when we feel lonely. Yet, all too often we forget to turn to God, which is the proper response to the problem of loneliness. Jesus has invited us to come to Him when the burden of loneliness is too much for us to bear.

"Come to me, all you who are weary and burdened, and I will give you rest. Take my yoke upon you and learn from me, for I am gentle and humble in heart, and you will find rest for your souls. For my yoke is easy and my burden is light."

Matthew 11:28–30

God is always there for you. He understands your need for friendship and fellowship. Loneliness is triggered when we lack connections with other people, but when we unite ourselves with others, we are much stronger together:

> Two are better than one, because they have a good return for their work:
> If one falls down, his friend can help him up. But pity the man who falls and has no one to help him up!
> Also, if two lie down together, they will keep warm. But how can one keep warm alone? Though one may be overpowered, two can defend themselves. A cord of three strands is not quickly broken.
>
> *Ecclesiastes 4:9-12*

God designed us to desire friendship and companionship and to find our greatest fulfilment in loving others. However, there are times when we feel very lonely, even when we have people around us. It is as if there is a gap in our souls. That is why we need to draw closer to God in times of loneliness.

Always believe that God is with you; and, when loneliness starts to creep in, turn to Him and away from yourself, for He alone is your comfort and refuge.

> Trust in him at all times… pour out your hearts to him, for God is our refuge.
>
> *Psalm 62:8*

Chapter 5

Causes of Loneliness

Loneliness can be the result of real aloneness or perceived isolation. Where you are really alone, you may not have any control over the cause of your situation; your only choice is how you will respond to it. You can respond in a mature way and become a stronger person; or you can react negatively to your "loneliness" and become anxious or bitter about it. You can accept it gracefully or you can fight it—which would be much like scratching a wound, resulting in more infection.

Perceived isolation may be due to the person suffering from low self-esteem or harboring negative attitudes. Unfavorable circumstances or the lack of meaningful relationships are other reasons.

Low Self-Esteem

People who suffer from poor self-esteem or who feel worthless tend to isolate themselves from others. When such people look in the mirror, they do not like what they see and they cannot bear to look at themselves for any length of time. This attitude makes it difficult for them to build a lasting relationship with anyone. So they isolate themselves and withdraw from the presence of others. But such behavior only serves to reinforce their feelings of loneliness.

Another reason for their isolating themselves is the fear of rejection. People with low self-esteem often withdraw from social situations that they believe will lead to their being rejected by others.

Thus, loneliness can become a lifestyle for the person who struggles with poorly developed social or interpersonal skills.

Negative Attitudes

Then there are those who harbor negative attitudes like self-pity, anger, fear and self-centeredness. Such people stand in danger of allowing an ever-deepening cycle of loneliness to sink itself into their souls, and this will make it next to impossible for others to befriend them.

Circumstances that Isolate Us

When we face situations like the death of a spouse, the breakup of a relationship, a divorce or singlehood, we can become vulnerable to loneliness. Other situations such as being handicapped or being a newcomer to an area, or even being exceptionally talented or wealthy, can cause us to be shunned by others.

Circumstances during our childhood or developmental years can cause some among us to become loners. For example, growing up with a cold, distant, or overly critical parent may make one shy away from intimacy with others. Some people have simply never learned to communicate well or to get along with their peers. Others have overly aggressive, intimidating or demanding personalities that make people withdraw from them.

Rejection by others is the form of loneliness that causes us the most pain. This is when you feel you have been betrayed or forsaken in your hour of need by those closest to you. Paul felt forsaken; he said of his trial before Nero:

> At my first defense, no one came to my support, but everyone deserted me.
>
> *2 Timothy 4:16*

Rejection is one of the most difficult experiences for us to handle, whether it is as children in the school playground, as a teenager at a party, or as a spouse in a marriage. That is why divorce is so painful and why God hates it. It is an act of abandoning and forsaking the partner to whom one has made a lifelong commitment.

> "I hate divorce," says the LORD God of Israel, "and I hate a man's covering himself with violence as well as with his garment," says the LORD Almighty.
> So guard yourself in your spirit, and do not break faith.
>
> *Malachi 2:16*

Some people try to deal with loneliness by becoming workaholics, but this will inevitably take its toll. Others try materialism; they buy up everything in sight. They think, "If I can just improve the 'quality' of my life, I will be happy." But things do not satisfy us for long. The fact is, you cannot buy happiness.

Some turn to alcohol or drugs. Others, married but still lonely, resort to having extramarital affairs. And then there are those who lose themselves in a fantasy world by reading novels, playing internet games, or watching television. But all of these are poor substitutes for a fulfilling relationship, and they take us further and further away from God's will for us.

Need for Personal Relationships

> The LORD God said, "It is not good for the man to be alone. I will make a helper suitable for him."
>
> *Genesis 2:18*

As the story of Adam and Eve illustrates, God wants us to share our lives with other people. The importance He places on personal relationships is evident from the amount of space devoted to it in the Bible. Both the Old and New Testaments have a lot to say about marriage, parenthood, friendship and church fellowship.

A variety of personal factors and other circumstances can sometimes short-circuit our ability to connect with others. Perhaps you have become insecure about meeting new people after the death of a loved one or a breakup with someone close to you. Maybe some social setbacks have led you to think that no one could possibly be interested in your company. Relocating to a new area may have left you longing for old friendships and unable to start new ones.

All these are obstacles to our forming meaningful relationships. If not dealt with promptly, they can cause us to experience long-term loneliness.

Need for Fellowship with God

We were created to find our ultimate fulfilment through intimate fellowship with our Creator. But, because of man's sin and rebellion, this fellowship has been severed.

Spiritual emptiness and an internal void are the results of a non-existent relationship with God.

> Then God said, "Let us make man in our image, in our likeness..." So God created man in his own image, in the image of God he created him.
>
> *Genesis 1: 26-27*

Human beings were made in God's image so that they would fulfill a role that was theirs alone; no other creature on earth could do it. We would have fellowship with God and be the objects of His love. This is the most important relationship of all, above every other relationship.

Yes, it is true that God wants us to develop meaningful relationships with our family and friends. But it is also clear from God's Word that there is one relationship which is dominant from His point of view: this is the fellowship He wants to have with us, which forms the foundation for all of our other relationships.

> A man of many companions may come to ruin, but there is a friend who sticks closer than a brother.
>
> *Proverbs 18:24*

You cannot always depend on people. We are all human and we will fail each other from time to time. But we can always depend on God. He is always with you and always near you. He will always love you. He is a friend you can trust and depend upon all the time. He is the Friend who sticks closer than a brother.

> For God has said, "I will never fail you. I will never forsake you."
>
> *Hebrews 13:5 (NLT)*

Chapter 6

Loneliness Is Different from Solitude

The New Testament Greek word *mono* means "single, alone, solitary". To be alone is to be solitary and to be separated from others. It is meant to be a positive experience. Jesus often sought to be alone. He separated Himself from others in order to commune alone with the Father.

> After he had dismissed them, he went up on a mountainside by himself to pray. When evening came, he was there alone...
>
> *Matthew 14:23*

Loneliness, on the other hand, involves a deep sense of isolation and disconnection from others. It happens to people when they feel that they have no one with whom to share the joys and hardships of life. Some say their loneliness feels less like sadness and more like an imprisonment that leaves them despondent towards life.

While everyone can benefit from a certain amount of "alone" time, all of us need close interpersonal relationships for a healthy and fulfilling life. Sadly, people today feel more isolated than ever before. The average family unit is severely fractured, the divorce rate is escalating, and more people are living alone today than at any time in the past.

How is Being Lonely Different from Being Alone?

- Loneliness is a state of the heart. It is an inner feeling of isolation or emptiness. It is a need to be with another person. But not everyone who is alone feels empty. There are people who prefer to be by themselves, and that does not mean they are lonely. You can be alone and yet be content with it.

- On the other hand, you can be in the midst of people and still feel lonely for any number of reasons. Perhaps you are desperately missing a loved one who is not with you. Or you are looking for someone to fill up your time or the emptiness in your heart. Or you might be longing for something that does not exist anymore or that has never existed in your life.

Loneliness is a negative state of the heart, where you are never satisfied with being by yourself and are always looking elsewhere for fulfilment. People most often encounter the destructive force of loneliness right after a separation or divorce or the breakup of a relationship—when the contact you had with the other person is no longer there, but you are left feeling empty and longing for it.

Loneliness has caused many people to turn to drugs or alcohol abuse, to become workaholics, to fall into adultery, fornication or gluttony (overeating), or to rush into finding a new love. All these are desperate attempts to fill the void in their hearts; but whenever such distractions are not available, feelings of loneliness creep in and start to torment them again.

Single people need to know that marriage or having kids is not the answer to loneliness. Do not marry someone because you feel lonely. Overcome your negative feelings first. Many people say, "When I get married, then I will be happy," or "When I have children, then I will be happy," or "When I have a nice family, a comfortable home, and a fulfilling, high-paying job, then I will be happy." They assume that they can't be happy until everything is perfect in their lives.

However, marriage or a good job does not guarantee happiness or an end to loneliness. Millions of married people are lonely too, and they are looking for understanding and acceptance from their spouse. Each heart knows its own bitterness, and no one can share its joy (*Proverbs 14:10*). Listen to King David as he pours out his heart to God:

> Turn to me and be gracious to me,
> for I am lonely and afflicted.
>
> *Psalm 25:16*

David was a king, yet he felt lonely. He had all those loyal subjects and people under him, but he still got lonely. In David's day, kings had many wives and concubines; but not even all of his wives and mistresses could cheer King David up when he was lonely. Instead, he turned to the Lord for the cure to his loneliness.

David knew that only God could satisfy the longings in his heart. He knew God would not let him down. Remember, it is possible to be alone and yet not be lonely. It is possible to be alone and still be happy. On the other hand, it is possible to be in the company of friends and still be lonely. It is possible to be married and still be lonely.

God cares for the lonely. He looks on them with grace and mercy. Instead of building walls we need to build bridges. We need to stop complaining, "God, I'm so lonely," and start saying, "God, help me be a friend to somebody today."

Love is the antidote to loneliness. Instead of waiting to be loved, take the initiative. Utilize your time, minimize your hurt, recognize God's presence, and empathize with others. Remember, the Lord Jesus Christ, the Son of God, knows what it is like to be lonely.

In His darkest hour, in the Garden of Gethsemane, while He prayed earnestly, His friends were all asleep. When the soldiers came to arrest Him, His friends deserted Him. When He was put on trial, His closest friend denied Him. On the cross, when Jesus was carrying the sins of the world on His shoulders, even His Father turned His face away from Him. Jesus cried out, "My God, my God, why have you forsaken me?" (*Mark 15:34*)

Yes, Jesus understands your loneliness. Let Christ help you conquer your loneliness as you turn to Him in prayer. Paul said, "But the Lord stood at my side and gave me strength." (*2 Timothy 4:17*). When Paul was physically alone and acutely lonely, God made His presence felt and gave Paul the strength to endure and press on despite his loneliness.

Where is God when you are lonely? *Right next to you.* Jesus said, "I will not leave you as orphans" (*John 14:18*). God the Father says, "Never will I leave you, never will I forsake you." (*Hebrews 13:5*). There is no place on earth where God is not present. As long as you understand this, you are never really alone.

Prayer is a great comfort in lonely times. When we find ourselves getting lonely, it is a sign that we need to talk to God and let Him talk to us; it is time for us to become better acquainted with God. If you want to overcome loneliness, you have to start to utilize your time, minimize your hurt, and recognize God's presence in your life.

Chapter 7

You Are Not Alone

People feel lonely for many reasons. If you are struggling with loneliness, you are not alone. Everyone experiences seasons of isolation for one reason or another, but we can all overcome feelings of loneliness by committing ourselves to God—as Jesus did in *Luke 23:46* when He called out with a loud voice, "Father, into your hands I commit my spirit."

Loneliness can be very painful. It can make you feel cut off, vulnerable and frightened. Jesus felt so lonely on the cross when His Father turned His back on Him (because of our sins that were laid upon Him as our Savior). On the cross, Christ lost all connection, not just with the disciples, but also with the Father.

Earlier on, when Jesus was betrayed by Judas, His disciples had deserted Him. They had left Jesus alone. Yet, even then, He had not felt lonely, for the Father was with Him (*John 16:32*). It was not until His Father turned His back on Him that Jesus felt all alone. He felt the pain of loneliness the very moment when God forsook him:

> And at the ninth hour Jesus cried out in a loud voice, *"Eloi, Eloi, lama sabachthani?"* —which means, "My God, my God, why have you forsaken me?"
>
> *Mark 15:34*

At one time or another, all of us have felt the need for companionship: for someone who will listen to us and reassure us; someone who will understand our deepest feelings and innermost thoughts. We need someone who can empathize with us and be sensitive to our emotions.

The good news is that there *is* someone who possesses all of these qualities; someone who understands our deepest thoughts and feelings, and who will listen to us, reassure us, and be sensitive to our emotions. He is none other than Jesus, the One who has overcome loneliness for you. He is saying to you today, just as much as He said these words to His disciples:

> "In this world you will have trouble. **But take heart! I have overcome the world."**
>
> *John 16:33*

Therefore since you have "a great high priest... Jesus the Son of God", hold firmly to the faith you profess. For you do not have a high priest who is unable to sympathize with your loneliness, but you have one who has been tempted in every way, just as you are, yet He was without sin (*Hebrews 4:14-15*).

No one—whether rich or poor, black or white, Christian or non-Christian—is exempt from the pain of loneliness. All who go through life have felt lonely at one time or another; however, it is how you react to your loneliness that determines the state of your emotional and spiritual health.

How happy or confident we are is directly proportionate to the degree that we surrender ourselves to God. When we do that, we can experience joy, peace and happiness in abundance, thereby limiting loneliness to the insignificant part it deserves.

Read the Bible and seek God in prayer, and He will, through His Holy Spirit in you, guide you as to what path to take next. Jesus has given us His Holy Spirit to be our Comforter, Counselor, Helper, Intercessor, Advocate and Strengthener, that He may remain with us forever.

Our Lord did not leave us as orphans; therefore, when you are lonely, a good thing to do is to pray. When you pray, you are no longer alone. Suddenly God's presence is there through the Holy Spirit. And it is good to pray when you are lonely because you can be honest with God about how you are feeling. What I mean is not the repetitive kind of prayer, but rather the opening of your heart to the Lord.

This is His personal invitation to you:

> Cast your cares on the LORD and he will sustain you; he will never let the righteous fall.
>
> *Psalm 55:22*

Being open with the Lord about your feelings, whatever they are, is very important. Oftentimes, we attempt to "hide" our weaknesses and walk away from God even more when we are most in need of Him.

Trust Him, that He will be the One to fill the void in you. God will fill you with a deep sense of satisfaction, something that no human being can ever give you. He is the One who created you and He knows you better than anyone else.

As King David so beautifully puts it:

O Lord, thou hast searched me, and known me. Thou knowest my downsitting and mine uprising, thou understandest my thought afar off.

Thou compassest my path and my lying down, and art acquainted with all my ways.

For there is not a word in my tongue, but, lo, O LORD, thou knowest it altogether.

Thou hast beset me behind and before, and laid thine hand upon me. Such knowledge is too wonderful for me; it is high, I cannot attain unto it.

Whither shall I go from thy spirit? Or whither shall I flee from thy presence? If I ascend up into heaven, thou art there: if I make my bed in hell, behold, thou art there.

If I take the wings of the morning, and dwell in the uttermost parts of the sea; Even there shall thy hand lead me, and thy right hand shall hold me.

If I say, Surely the darkness shall cover me; even the night shall be light about me. Yea, the darkness hideth not from thee; but the night shineth as the day: the darkness and the light are both alike to thee.

Psalm 139: 1-11 (KJV)

Whatever may be causing you to feel lonely, there is a way out. It begins with confronting the root cause of your loneliness, which every human being must come to terms with: that is, the spiritual loneliness of being separated from God.

Each of us has a need to connect with something larger than ourselves in order to fill the spiritual vacuum that exists within us all.

The Bible is God's plan for developing the most important relationship in our lives: friendship with God. When we accept Jesus Christ as our Savior and obey His Word, we enter into communion with the Creator of the universe. God Almighty will use His Word to heal us and He will place His Holy Spirit within us.

> This is my comfort and consolation in my affliction: that Your word has revived me and given me life.
>
> *Psalm 119:50 (AMP)*

Jesus refers to the Holy Spirit as the "Counselor" (*John 14:16*) who will guide us into all truth (*John 16:13*). The Apostles Paul and John tell us that God's Spirit will fill us with assurance of our membership in His family (*Romans 8:16; 1 John 4:13*).

Day by day, through prayer and Bible reading, we can experience the wonderful fellowship that God wants to have with each of His children. He is never too busy to listen. It should be the goal of every one of us to devote ourselves to the Lord in both body and spirit. This will enable us to close any back door that can allow loneliness to creep into our lives.

As the proverb says, "Idle minds are the devil's playground". This means that, if you do not keep yourself busy with the things of God, the devil will flood you with his garbage. Devote yourself to prayer, and God will fill the void in your heart with His presence. Devote yourself to God and serve Him faithfully, for He is a Holy God.

Get rid of sin. You cannot expect God to come into your heart while you devote yourself to the devil. Every seed of the enemy sown in your soul has the potential to cripple your relationship with God. This is what the Bible calls "the little foxes that ruin the vineyards" (*Song of Solomon 2:15*).

> The widow who is really in need and left all alone puts her hope in God and continues night and day to pray and to ask God for help. But the widow who lives for pleasure is dead even while she lives.
>
> *1 Timothy 5:5*

Devotion to prayer is the solution for every single person on earth. But living for pleasure will lead you to death. If we live by the Spirit we will not gratify the desires of the sinful nature. Yield to the Holy Spirit, trust in Him, and rely upon Him to give you victory over loneliness. Then you will be fruitful in every area of your life.

A dynamic walk with God is a solid foundation for building relationships with others. As God's children, we are members of an incredibly large, extended family that encompasses the whole world. Christians who do not go to church or do not get involved in church activities cut themselves off from a rich source of companionship.

As a Christian, ask yourself if you are spending regular quality time with your Heavenly Father! Are you active in a local church? Ask God to lead you into a deeper relationship with Him and greater involvement with fellow believers.

Chapter 8

How to Overcome Loneliness

All of us have a choice as to how we live our life after losing a loved one—whether this loss was due to death, divorce, or any other reason. After we lose a loved one, the quality of our new life depends upon the choices we make. After all, life is about choices.

Your choices can either imprison you in the past or transform you into a new person. They can bind you and make you a captive to your fears and regrets, or they can lead you to a deeper relationship with God. As a survivor, you must embrace the new life with all of its promises and hopes. Otherwise, you could become paralyzed by fear and loneliness.

You must become a new person: not dependent upon your past relationships, but drawing upon the strength you have received from them. Never allow yourself to be disabled by your past; instead, choose to draw on your inner strength to build a new life for yourself.

Life goes on. The passing away of the old invariably makes way for the birth of new life:

> At least there is hope for a tree:
> > If it is cut down, it will sprout again, and its new shoots will not fail.
> >
> > Its roots may grow old in the ground and its stump die in the soil, yet at the scent of water it will bud and put forth shoots like a plant.
>
> *Job 14: 7-9*

It is very important to be open and honest with God about the wound that is causing the loneliness and to "bring it to His table".

The Bible tells us to cast our cares upon the Lord (*Psalm 55:22*). Why? Because He CARES for us. He wants to be a part of what we are going through. He wants to be right there by our side when we are facing loneliness!

We need to include God in our struggles with loneliness! Jesus is very familiar with all the weaknesses that you and I face, and He actually desires to be involved in our battles. Ask Him for the courage to reach out to others and try new things. Trust God to give you what He wants you to have: an abundant life that includes intimate and faithful friends.

You will need God's power to strengthen you in your inner being through the Holy Spirit. Christ and His Word must also dwell in you so that you can be grounded and rooted in love. Get rid of all bitterness, rage and anger, brawling and slander, along with every form of malice; and be kind and compassionate towards others, and forgive them—just as, in Christ, God forgave you (*Ephesians 4:32*).

Loneliness is not conquered by external forces; the healing must come from within. Loneliness must be broken the way it was formed—one act at a time. You must begin by repeatedly choosing not to react negatively to your inner weaknesses. And do not expect your negative attitudes to disappear in one miraculous moment when you pray at the altar. In the same way that a negative habit is formed by small repeated actions, so is spiritual victory achieved through repeated obedience to God.

So, do not pray for God to take you out of your desert by some supernatural miracle. God can and may do it, but usually He does not. Instead, start looking into the Word of God to find answers. Then, listen with your own "inner ear" to hear what God is saying to you.

> Great peace have they who love your law and nothing can make them stumble.
>
> *Psalm 119:165*

Steps to Overcoming Loneliness

Loneliness cannot be cured but it can be overcome. It is up to you to take the following steps to break free from its grip.

1. Admit that there is a problem

You need, first of all, to admit that you have a problem. It is only when you have acknowledged your loneliness that you can take steps to escape from it.

Sometimes when a loved one dies, your brain shuts down. You cannot think, and you do not know what to say. Shock sets in. You cannot control your emotions and you begin to grieve over the person. You cry, scream or yell. Grief is outward, like the bursting of a tire. It is easy to recognize because we can see its obvious display of suffering, agony, and the flood of emotions it brings. Meanwhile, mourning is inward; it is like a slow puncture, like a silent death. Grief is usually manifested for a short period; but mourning can go on unseen for a long time, with far-reaching effects that persist long after the beloved's death.

Sarah was 127 years old when she died (*Genesis 23:1*). The Bible describes the two-fold reaction of Abraham: "Abraham went to mourn [inwardly] for Sarah and to weep [grieve outwardly] for her." (*Genesis 23:2, AMP*) Abraham wept outwardly for Sarah—he grieved. He also mourned inwardly; and he probably harbored questions such as: "Why her of all people?" or "How can I live without her?"

It is only natural to grieve and mourn when we lose a loved one. Jesus wept when his friend Lazarus died (*John 11:35*). He was not ashamed to show His feelings, and neither should we withhold our tears. In fact, expressing our emotions helps us deal with the death of a loved one; and the more deeply we deal with our loss, the quicker we are healed.

There might be times when our loneliness gets unbearable and we become stuck in our grief. When this happens, seeking help from professionals is tangible demonstration of our courage and a sign that we are ready to rebuild our lives.

We are lonely because no one can take the place of our beloved. We can never replace them with anyone else. But we can best commemorate their memories by taking care of ourselves, and by reaching out and connecting with others.

2. Resolve to move on

Evaluate your life honestly in the light of God's Word. Accept what you cannot change. The death of a spouse, a divorce, relocation away from old friends, and other unalterable circumstances must be faced squarely. God can use changes in our lives to open doors to new experiences, but we must be willing to let go of the past and move on.

Let us look at Abraham again. Notice the things he did to get on with his life after the death of his wife. First, he made a physical detachment from the body: "Then Abraham rose from beside his dead wife." (*Genesis 23:3*)

The second thing he did was to make preparations to purchase the burial plot. He went to the Hittites and said, "Give me property for a burial place among you, that I may bury my dead out of my sight." (*Genesis 23:4, AMP*) They negotiated the price of the land for quite a while, but eventually Abraham paid the price and bought his first piece of property in the Promised Land.

Abraham then took another step to let go of the past and MOVE ON with his life: "Abraham again took a wife, and her name was Keturah." (*Genesis 25:1, NKJV*) This does not mean that everyone who has lost a spouse should marry again. But, it does give permission to the surviving spouse to go on living and, in some cases, to marry again. Your "Keturah" could be a new career, a new community, or a new relationship. It is time you buried the past out of sight and MOVE ON with your life.

> Forget the former things; do not dwell on the past. See, I am doing a new thing! Now it springs up; do you not perceive it? I am making a way in the desert and streams in the wasteland.
> *Isaiah 43: 18-19*

Life does not end when our beloved dies or when there's a divorce. We do not diminish our memories of our loved ones when we experience moments of serenity, joy and quietude after they are gone.

We have to learn to move on, no matter what the situation might be. This is hard to do, but we need to break our attachment to the dead and move on with our lives. Many people relive the agony of the death; they retell—to everyone they meet—the story of how the person died; they constantly go back to visit the grave; they refuse to remove the clothes and other belongings of the beloved from the home. What they are doing is hanging on to the past. But there must be a detachment; life must go on.

3. Minimize the pain and bitterness

The next step is to minimize the hurt. Play down the loneliness. Do not exaggerate it, and do not rehash it over and over again. Stop telling yourself, "I'm so lonely, I'm so lonely."

Do not allow the loneliness to make you bitter, and do not allow resentment to build up in your life. Resentment only makes you lonelier. The Apostle Paul said, "At my first defense, no one came to my support, but everyone deserted me. May it not be held against them" (*2 Timothy 4:16*).

Paul demonstrated that he wanted to forgive those who had hurt him. He wanted to be free from bitterness. Bitterness only locks you up in a self-imposed prison and drives people away from you. It causes you to complain constantly and be suspicious of others. This definitely does not make you a pleasant person to have around.

When Paul said, "May it not be held against them," he wanted to be a better person, not a bitter person. The choice is yours, whether to remain bitter towards life, God and others, or to become better by letting go of resentment. We can choose to really live, even if we are alone. Aloneness only becomes loneliness when the separation makes us forever sad and dejected.

> See, I have set before you this day life and good, and death and evil.
>
> *Deuteronomy 30:15 (AMP)*

In *John 11: 1-44*, we read the story of two sisters and their brother Lazarus. Lazarus had died and his sisters, Mary and Martha, had buried him in a tomb not too far from their house. When Jesus came to them after the burial, both ladies said, "Lord, if you had been here, my brother would not have died." (*John 11:21, 32*) This was a statement that the two sisters had been repeating between themselves since Lazarus died.

In their grief and mourning, they had somewhat blamed their brother's death on Jesus. They kept reminding themselves that Jesus was a miracle worker and, if only He had come on time, He could have saved Lazarus from dying. But Jesus had His reasons for not showing up earlier. He wanted to demonstrate that He came to earth to overcome death itself and not just to prevent it.

God knows the best plan for everyone. As with Lazarus, He might have allowed your loved one to die or that tragic incident to happen. He did not prevent it. Why? So that He could demonstrate His power to resurrect the dead.

God can overcome death. Jesus said, "I am the resurrection and the life. He who believes in me will live, even though he dies." (*John 11:25*) Therefore, look beyond death or whatever the cause of your loneliness may be, to the resurrection of your hopes and the new life that God has in store for you. Let go of bitterness over what you have lost, and let God give you His plan for your life.

4. Change what can be changed

Sometimes it is possible to alter the circumstances that cause us to be lonely. In such cases, you owe it to yourself to take whatever measures are necessary to change your situation. Face the problem head-on and change what can be changed.

If we stay alone too long, our homes will become protective shells shielding us from having to confront reality. Some struggle with loneliness but refuse to ask for help because they are afraid of "burdening" friends and family with their problems. Others are afraid of looking "weak"; they think they should be able to take care of everything themselves.

We need to let go of all these unfounded fears and step out boldly to seek help from others. Start slowly—make one or two phone calls a day. Begin to develop relationships with new friends. One baby step at a time.

5. Develop self-esteem

Stop all destructive self-talk, such as telling yourself that you are unlikable. Remember: He who guards his lips guards his life, but he who speaks rashly will come to ruin. (*Proverbs 13:3*) Your tongue has the power of life and death. (*Proverbs 18:21*)

Read the Word of God. Then you will be able to bring forth good things out of the good stored up in you. For out of the abundance of the heart, the mouth speaks. If your heart is full of bitterness, this is what your mouth will spew out. No one has to open up your heart to find out what is inside you. Just your speech is enough! Each time you open your mouth, you let the world see what is inside you. If your heart is full of God's Word, your mouth will speak life to yourself and to others.

6. Make the best of every situation

If life gives you a lemon, make lemonade. In other words, make the best of even the worst situation. Resist the temptation to give up and do nothing. Loneliness tends to paralyze a person. Lonely people often ignore their own needs and do not take care of themselves. They do not eat right, and they do not exercise. They just sit around and do nothing. Paul resisted that temptation. When he was lonely in prison, he refused to sit down and mope.

> When you come, bring the cloak that I left with Carpus at Troas, and my scrolls, especially the parchments.
>
> *2 Timothy 4:13*

Paul decided that, if he could not visit the churches, he could still write to them. He made the best of his situation. In the same way, if you cannot be where the action is, you can still do something from wherever you are. God can use your loneliness for good.

Many of Paul's important letters might never have been written had he not been in prison. If he had been able to travel freely, he would have visited the churches and preached to the early Christians instead of writing to them. But, because he was imprisoned, he decided to write those inspired letters that now form an essential part of our New Testament—and have since blessed Christians around the world for the last two thousand years and more.

By turning adversity into advantage, the Apostle Paul multiplied his ministry a thousand fold. So, if you find yourself alone, utilize your time wisely instead of falling a prey to despondency.

7. Get rid of negative attitudes

We cannot alleviate loneliness until we have dealt with the root cause of it, which can often be traced to our negative attitudes. These attitudes erect barriers in our life instead of bridges, and we have to get rid of them. You must resolutely rid yourself of all the negative thoughts that are alienating you from others, and you must also sincerely ask the Lord to cleanse you of destructive thoughts.

Unless you correct your negative attitudes, you will not be able to move on. Your negative thoughts will stand before you like a barrier. When Abram was harboring negative attitudes concerning God's promises to him, God had to tell him to go out at night to count the stars. He did this in order to turn the man's negative thoughts around.

God had promised Abram a son but Abram doubted God. It was only when he began numbering the stars that he could visualize the number of descendants he would eventually have. Once he got rid of his negative attitudes, he began to have a new perspective on God's promises. Instead of a barrier, he began to build bridges—positive thoughts—that allowed him to move on.

> And Abram said, "You have given me no children; so a servant in my household will be my heir."
> Then the word of the LORD came to him: "This man will not be your heir, but a son who is your own flesh and blood will be your heir."
> He took him outside and said, "Look up at the sky and count the stars—if

indeed you can count them." Then he said to him, "So shall your offspring be."

Abram believed the LORD, and he credited it to him as righteousness.

Genesis 15: 3-6

One widow told her therapist, "It is hard going solo." The therapist helped her to gain a new perspective when he asked, "What do you like about living alone?"

She paused, and then answered, "I do not have to worry about his health every second. I am free to travel. I enjoy working as a volunteer at my local hospice. And I am learning to treasure my alone time."

Then she smiled and said, "Now, I can even put mushrooms in my spaghetti sauce. My husband hated mushrooms. I love them." Though it is hard to go solo, there is a positive side to it: you can do the things you have always wanted to do, and there is no one to stop you.

Focus on your strengths. Too often people make the mistake of focusing on their weaknesses. They think they must begin at their weakest point to make themselves strong. But, think about it this way: What will you get if you begin with your weaknesses?

You will only get weakness from your weaknesses. So, begin with your strengths. Work from the strongest areas of your life to the weakest. Then you will draw strength from your strengths.

8. Stand up to your fears

Fear can raise its head in many forms: for example, we may fear being hurt, rejected or intimidated by others. Such fears can reinforce our loneliness if we give way to them. But, when we challenge those same fears by seeking a release through Christ and His Word, we are well on our way to overcoming loneliness.

> For God has not given us a spirit of fear, but of power and of love and of a sound mind.
>
> 2 Timothy 1:7 (NKJV)

9. Challenge your feelings of inferiority

Deliberately challenge any feelings of inferiority you may be harboring. One of Satan's greatest lies is the thought he tries to put into us—that we are of no value. However, the Bible tells us that we are of great value to God (*1 Corinthians 7:23; 1 Corinthians 12: 14-27; Matthew 6:26; Psalm 139:17*). So, resist any thoughts of inferiority by standing upon the reality of who you are in Christ.

> [Jesus] replied, "Every plant that my heavenly Father has not planted will be pulled up by the roots."
>
> *Matthew 15:13*

Feelings of inferiority and loneliness are not from God, and therefore they should be pulled up by the roots through the power of the Holy Spirit. For it is not by might nor by power, but by the Spirit of the LORD (*Zechariah 4:6*) that we will be able to overcome the works of the Enemy.

10. Establish a schedule and keep to it

Establish a daily or weekly schedule and keep to it. Loneliness often seems more intense when we have nothing to do. Organize your time and be sure to include some outdoor activities as well as quiet moments for self-reflection. Start exercising regularly and make the most of your moments of solitude.

Start exercising regularly

Take walks around your neighborhood, a local park or a shopping mall. Take an interest in what is happening around you, and talk to people you meet. You will start to feel better physically and emotionally.

Make the most of your time alone

Aloneness (as opposed to loneliness) can be a very positive experience. Aloneness, or solitude, gives us a chance to reflect on our lives, to meditate on God's will for us, and to find healing for the wounds inflicted by the world.

11. Go out and make new friends

Often, all that is required to escape loneliness is the determination to seek out new friends. Shyness and the fear of rejection are usually the biggest hurdles to initiating a friendship; but we mustn't allow ourselves to be intimidated by these hindrances. We must take the initiative to reach out to others. If we want to have friends, we must show ourselves to be friendly (*Proverbs 18:24*).

Relationships do not just happen. We have to invest time and effort to develop them. Notice what God told Elijah to do in 1 Kings Chapter 19:

> "Go… anoint Hazael as king over Syria. Also you shall anoint Jehu the son of Nimshi as king over Israel."
>
> *1 Kings 19: 15-16 (NKJV)*

God told Elijah to GO and meet those people; He did not bring Hazael or Jehu into Elijah's life. So, if you are lonely, do not just pray for a friend. Go and find one! Put feet to your prayers. God gave Elijah positive tasks to do: he had to leave the desert—walk—until he found the men he was to anoint for ministry. God did not send the men to find Elijah in the desert.

God will probably not send someone to rescue you in your lonely room or your deserted desert. Instead, you will have to get up and go out to meet a new friend, pastor, ministry or support group!

It is time you left your self-made desert. Get up and get out of your self-pity. God will probably not work a miracle to get you out of your self-imprisonment; He wants you to take the initiative to step out by yourself.

To break out of your negative habit of self-imposed isolation, visualize yourself doing positive things for people—for example, look for a new realm of service, look out for people in need. It is good to picture yourself helping others. When you do, you are seeing yourself as God wants you to be. When we serve others, friendship will be the result.

> And let us not neglect our meeting together, as some people do, but encourage one another, especially now that the day of his return is drawing near.
>
> *Hebrews 10:25 (NLT)*

One of the best ways to overcome loneliness is to go to church and make a lot of great friends there: the ones you can call upon if you need someone to talk to or to encourage you; the people who will be genuinely concerned for your wellbeing, who can teach you from their own life experiences, and who share the same faith as you do. You will have so much in common with these people; it would be hard to be lonely when you are meeting friends in church all the time.

Another thing you can do to overcome loneliness is to invite friends over for fellowship. Invite them to your home for lunch or tea or just to enjoy a good time together. Spend time chitchatting with your friends or have everyone take part in wholesome, fun activities together.

Don't just sit around, staring at the TV or newspaper all day. The media is the most common weapon the Enemy is using to influence our lives negatively. You watch a show and you start to imagine yourself as one of the characters—usually the hero or heroine. And a void is created in your heart.

The next thing you know, you get depressed and lonely, and start looking for someone or something to fill the emptiness in your heart. You will be longing for something that does not exist in real life but only in a fantasy world.

God created us for relationships, and it is up to us to find ways to meet those relational needs. Get busy serving others! Christians suffer from loneliness because they are sitting instead of serving.

12. Cultivate your relationship with God

Practice looking at yourself from God's viewpoint. Study the Scriptures and meditate on verses that illustrate how much God values His children.

> Can a mother forget the baby at her breast and have no compassion on the child she has borne?
>
> Though she may forget, I will not forget you! See, I have engraved you on the palms of my hands; your walls are ever before me.
>
> *Isaiah 49: 15-16*

An intimate relationship with Christ is necessary for us to overcome loneliness. Do not look to people for fulfilment. Only Jesus can heal you of the pain of inner loneliness. Our Lord wants us to draw so close to His heart that we can share a meal with Him. He wants us to have communion with Him.

> Behold, I stand at the door and knock. If anyone hears My voice and opens the door, I will come in to him and dine with him, and he with Me.
>
> *Revelation 3:20 (NKJV)*

It is better to take refuge in the Lord than to trust in people (*Psalm 118:9*). Stop trusting in people in your times of loneliness, for that will only put your life under a curse. You will be like a person naked and destitute in the desert; you will not see any good come to you, but you will dwell in the parched places of the wilderness, in a salt land where no one lives—that is, in lonely circumstances (*Jeremiah 17:6*).

> This is what the LORD says: Cursed is the one who trusts in man, who depends on flesh for his strength and whose heart turns away from the LORD.
>
> *Jeremiah 17:5*

But blessed is the man who trust in the LORD, whose confidence is in him. He will be like a tree planted by the water that sends out its roots by the stream.

It does not fear when heat comes; its leaves are always green. It has no worries in a year of drought and never fails to bear fruit.

Jeremiah 17: 7-8

Above all, develop a closer relationship with God. Seek firs His kingdom and His righteousness, and the rest will come to you as a bonus (*Matthew 6:33*). No human love exists that can fill the void in you; it is only God's love that can satisfy you.

Lean on, trust in, and be confident in the Lord with all your heart and mind and do not rely on your own insight or understanding.

Proverbs 3:5 (AMP)

As you put your trust in God, you will be like a tree planted by the water, that spreads out its roots by the stream of the Holy Spirit. You will receive joy, peace and comfort from His presence. You will not fear when misfortune comes, and your life will always be in bloom. You will have no worries in times of loneliness, and you will never fail to bear the fruit of the Spirit.

****

If you have never invited Jesus Christ to be your Savior, now is a good time to do so. Making Jesus the Lord of your life will put you on a path that leads to intimacy with God, new friendships with fellow Christians in this life, and an eternal place in God's presence in the life hereafter.

If you want Jesus to be your Lord and Savior, simply say the prayer on page 99.

Prayer to Jesus

Dear Jesus, I know I am a sinner, and
I come before you humbly and ask
You to come into my life.
I ask for forgiveness for all my sins,
for I know that all have sinned and
fallen short of Your glory.

Come into my heart right now and be
the Lord of my heart and life.
Guide me on the right path and lead
me in Your ways, that I may live a
life that is pleasing to You and that
reflects Your love to others.
Make me Your child now, I pray in
Your precious Holy Name.

Amen.

If you have just prayed the prayer on page 99,

WELCOME TO THE FAMILY OF GOD!

Find a church that preaches God's Word, where you can grow in the Lord.

God bless you now and always.

Pastor Sydney Dikwi

Questions? Comments?

Write to Pastor Sydney Dikwi

Email: pastorsidneydikwi@yahoo.com
pastorsydneyd@gmail.com

Telephone: (+27) 71 008 4127
(+27) 71 470 2034

www.ingramcontent.com/pod-product-compliance
Lightning Source LLC
Chambersburg PA
CBHW031408040426
42444CB00005B/465